The Beauty in Our Differences

To my baby, Logan.
You can do anything. Mommy loves you.

My neighbor is the fastest runner I know.

So fast, that I have to squint just to get a glimpse of her as she speeds by.

Although I love to run with her, I can never keep up.

She dreams of one day winning an Olympic gold medal.
I believe she will.

When she finally stops to catch her breath,
some may notice her hearing aid.

It sits on the outside of her ears to help her hear sounds that she may miss.

My classmate is one of the smartest kids I know.

He likes every subject in school
and always has his hand raised high.

He helps everyone with their homework
and is always willing to stay after school.

In class, he takes out a small case.

He wears glasses that help him see things that are far away.

He may look a little different to some, but to us
he is just Isaac.

My buddy is the most talented musician I know.

When he picks up a violin, he fills the air
with beautiful sounds.

Everyone stands around in amazement
as the marvelous music rises.

Occasionally, people may take a curious glance.

His wheelchair helps him move independently
when he has trouble walking.

Others may take a second look, but to us
he is just Leo.

My friends say I am the kindest boy they know.

I like to get to know people from all walks of life.

I do this because the best part about friendship is learning about the beauty in our differences.

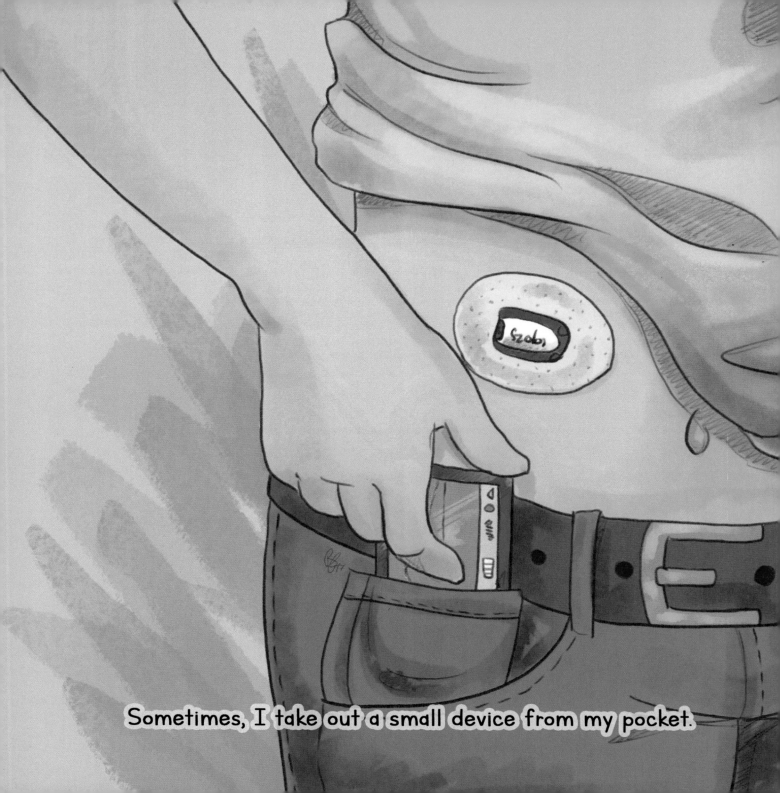

Sometimes, I take out a small device from my pocket.

A device that monitors blood sugar in people like me
with Type I Diabetes.

I may look a little different to some, but to my friends
I am just... Owen.

Everyone is unique and everyone has a story.

Made in the USA
Las Vegas, NV
06 June 2021